THE AMY AWARD
ANTHOLOGY 2

THE AMY AWARD
ANTHOLOGY 2

The Shortlisted Stories of the 2022 International
Amy MacRae Award for Memoir

SELECTED BY
ELIZABETH ROSNER

The Amy Award Anthology 2

Copyright 2023 by Alison Wearing

ISBN: 978-1-7781402-2-8

All rights reserved.

Editor: Alison Wearing

Book Designer: DigiWriting

Printed and bound in Canada.

The author greatly appreciates you taking the time to read this work. Please consider leaving a review wherever you bought the book, or telling your friends or blog readers about *The Amy Award Anthology 2* to help spread the word. Thank you for your support.

TABLE OF CONTENTS

The *International Amy MacRae Award for Memoir*
is given to an exceptional work of memoir writing.

The annual contest was created in celebration
of the life of Amy MacRae and in support of
her living legacy to improve the outcomes of
women with ovarian cancer.

This anthology showcases the shortlisted stories
from the 2022 contest, selected by this year's
judge, Elizabeth Rosner.

For more about this contest and the woman who
inspired it, please turn to the endnotes of this
book, or visit www.amyaward.com.

FIELD TRAJECTORIES: A TRIPTYCH

BY RAYYA LIEBICH, WINNER

Véronique 1978 – ?

You weren't sure what to think about the new girl with the rat tail who bragged about the metal detector at her old school. Your friendship grew out of fear and awe, an unlikely match of rainbow and black. The first time it happened was in seventh grade. It was spring, you were kissing a boy on the lush grass so you let the rumours about her whisper in the green. She came back to school with bandages on both wrists. But she didn't explain. Maybe there was nothing to say? A small patch of darkness grew between you.

Across a field of middle school memories, you'll never forget how the day Kurt Cobain died, she charged you in a hug. You let your tears roll down the back of her leather jacket. She held you upright and time stood still. How safe you felt in those tough arms. Safer here than on the grass, flirting with boys barely taller than you. You would return to this moment in your mind as proof that she could be there for you. With all the times she bailed, stood you up, forgot, you forced yourself to remember that she could be a good friend. She didn't mean to sabotage everything. She would eventually apologize.

The second time was different. You were in high school now. Fifteen? Does it matter? A classmate called you, and you ran to her house. You remember her swollen eyes not wanting to meet yours as if predicting your disapproval. She muttered a series of slurred *I'm sorrys*. You recoiled when she whispered your nickname: *Rainbow*. But five steps back, you could still see the pill bottles by her bedside. Two standing upright like pawns, one lying on its side. Checkmate. The jingle of her mother's keys in the door was your cue, and you bolted. That night you held the telephone to your ear and let it ring and ring and ring. Punishing yourself for your silence, imagining her in the hospital bed, shadows of a flatline painting white walls.

She survived. The friendship didn't. Years and years and years later, you would receive a letter in your cubicle at work, the handwriting instantly recognizable. How did she find this address? You were across the world from home and hadn't communicated with her in years. An A.A. assignment, she wrote you an apology for all the times she had been selfish, manipulative, dramatic, deceiving, destructive. She listed moments you had long forgotten—or had tried to. You were a young woman now, dressed in nice clothes at your first real job. But you still didn't have the tools to deal with this. Maybe you hadn't forgiven yourself yet for your silence. You folded the letter and sealed it back in the envelope. You searched for the courage to scrawl: *Return to sender*.

* * *

Marie 1979-1996

We moved by echolocation. Across the November field, we fluttered in black trench coats like bats, shielded from the sight of a flag at half-mast. We clung to each other to survive the vacant chair in homeroom, the empty locker in the hallway, the extra parking stall by the gate. At night, we filled our lungs with smoke and howled like a pack of wolves under shattered stars. All of us nocturnal now, we endured hours of staring at white ceilings in our own floating beds. Time bending as we watched sunlight skim our curtains, counting shadows like minutes until we could reunite with our clan.

Where were the adults? I remember crying on my mother's lap when I came home from school that day. Had the principal called all the parents to tell them about the accident? My mother let me slip away to my friend's house for what would be the first night of vigil. The next day at school, I remember which teachers addressed the loss and which ones didn't. Silently, I categorized in two: worthy of respect or hypocrite. Quadratic equations, iambic pentameter, the third person plural in German. White letters scratched on blackboards in a world that no longer existed.

The only meaningful gesture was from our theatre teacher. He shifted with discomfort carrying a tray of tea from the cafeteria and let us collapse in a heap on the empty stage. He gave us permission to speak, sit in silence, or wail. Some of us did all three. Awkwardly, he hovered by the door at the end of the day and offered to hug us goodbye.

Later in life, I wrote him a letter. It was one of the many *Thank You* cards I wrote after my mother died of ovarian cancer to acknowledge those who showed up for me. Perhaps an attempt to make up for those who hadn't. His kindness on the darkest day of my adolescence came to me so strongly, I felt compelled to reach out. I addressed him by his teacher name, though I must have been the same age that he had been as my teacher then. He replied in a long letter revealing his own experience with loss at seventeen, admitting he still felt haunted by witnessing a friend drown so many years ago. He recalled feeling utterly helpless as an adult in our world, but his loss had taught him that all he could do was sit with us in the circle of sorrow.

I could list bitter blame and reasons why so many of our lives went sideways after that year. The friends who didn't finish high school. The ones who never learned to drive. Those who could never get their addictions under control. I was one of the lucky ones. I carried my grief across the world to start a fresh life. But unlike my new peers, I felt the hollowness of loss in my bones. Like a flightless bird, I was always scanning the sky for my flock.

* * *

Dawson 1999-2017

I cross the snowy field and enter the high school. Familiar. Unfamiliar. Teens slither in as the bell rings and slump into their seats. I wonder which desk was his. Twenty years since I was in their shoes, a lifetime of preparation for this moment. But the rawness is palpable. Grief trickles down the back of my throat as I introduce myself and disclaim I'm not a counsellor. I'm just someone who has survived loss. I tell them grief is chaotic. Suicide is unbearably confusing. Adults in the world are so filled with discomfort, no one knows what to do. I tell them all feelings are allowed, and that sometimes writing helps. I ask them to pick up a pencil and do the impossible.

They write about how things should have been. How this is not it. I tell them I knew him. Their pencils pause in midflight, and they look up at me with shattered eyes. I tell them a long time ago I was his teacher. He was always making jokes and disrupting my lessons. Later, when my mother died and I went overseas, he had taken care of my dog. He had always wanted a dog, and this was his chance to show his parents how responsible he was. Unfortunately, the dog was terrified of thunder and within days in his care there had been a summer storm. My dog destroyed his mattress, their family sofa, and his mother's best sheets. I tell them how a few weeks ago he had filled up my car at the gas station, and how I had marvelled at how grown up he was. How well he looked. I tell them it's nobody's fault.

They write about all the things he loved, and who he might have become. Finally, they write a letter: *If you could read this letter, this is what I would say.* They find the courage to write his name: *Dear Dawson.* I pass out white envelopes weaving my way up and down aisles of loss. They write until the bell goes, then lick the envelopes closed. I stand by the door and find the courage to meet their eyes. They trickle out like a row of ducklings. Awkward and shuffling, protecting each other down the narrow hallway. I watch until they are out of sight, silently repeating: *you are not alone. You are not alone. You are not alone.*

PREPARING FOR LIFT-OFF

BY SUSANNA RANCE,
WINNER: PEOPLE'S CHOICE AWARD

Stepping into the kitchen, I unload my backpack onto the wooden chair near the door. The red wall by the window throws a pinkish hue onto the white wall opposite. My son Amaru looks up to greet me from the table where he's making pizza for our supper. He has a slight frown on his face, and his hand shakes as he points to a broken plant pot and clumps of earth that have fallen on the floor. Amaru is 36, and I'm in my seventieth year. Two years ago, he was diagnosed with an advanced brain tumour that makes his speech fragmented and affects his memory and movement. When he got ill, he gave up his job and home in Bolivia where he was born and moved back to London to live with me. I stopped working too and became a different kind of mother, accompanying him with an intensity I hadn't known since he was small.

It's the first of November, Day of the Dead, a time for opening up to death and dying. In Bolivia it's called *Todos Santos*, All Souls, and it's celebrated with home altars and rituals in graveyards and cemeteries. People use painted plaster masks to adorn bread for the dead. We don't have those in London, but we still follow the tradition of moulding sticky yellow dough into shapes of bowler-hatted *cholita*-ladies with wide skirts, llamas, and ladders to help the souls of the departed climb up to heaven. Above our kitchen table with its offerings of food and flowers, the wall is decorated with photos of loved ones pegged to silvery cords that sway when the air moves, like the souls passing through.

It doesn't take long for Amaru to get back to his usual good humour. He turns away from the pizza-making to share something more exciting: a video he's made on his cell phone.

"Look at this, Mum!"

There he is, on a grey-and-white speckled screen, wearing a baggy astronaut suit and a round helmet. He's flying around wide-eyed with a glassy expression. As I see him floating through, I peer into the background and glimpse views of his bed strewn with boxes, clothing, and hangers. Ghostly electronic music is playing. He's inside what looks like a space capsule, framed by a porthole with rough edges. The astronaut puts up his hand to the screen and turns off the film.

"What on earth...? Where did you get that suit?"

"From a beekeeper website. It arrived today. And this..."

Amaru shows me a clip-on device, a fish-eye lens that puts an adjustable circle on his mobile screen, making the scene look concave and mysterious. We go into his room, and now I can see how he filmed it as part of a space odyssey with himself as explorer. A silver wheely suitcase, open on his bed, contains gifts and a few items of clothing, with space for random objects. We're getting ready for a real-life journey later this month on flights that will take thirty hours to get us to La Paz, Bolivia. There's a sense of urgency in packing for the infinite. Amaru has already made it past the fourteen-month life expectancy for patients with his condition. He's strong in many ways, but we know he's living on borrowed time.

Amaru's spacesuit and helmet are piled on his bedroom table with a pair of white goatskin gloves, huge and scientific-looking. He shows me a webpage with images of beekeepers wearing serious expressions, bees sticking to their arms and dotted around them. He thinks the suit's too big, and he might have to exchange it. It's worth getting it right because this is the costume for the flying-around-without-gravity scenes, his journey into a new galaxy. I'm thinking that from here or from Bolivia, it's the same place he'll travel to, the same ejection of a human body, one small person, into the unknown.

Amaru wants the astronaut video to go into the film he's making with his soulmate Mila about his journey through illness and beyond. Some of the scenes will be in the memorial space he's setting up in Bolivia for relatives and friends to visit after he's gone. It's a kind of personal museum, a little room full of treasured objects, clothing, books, photos, musical instruments, and mementos from different passages in his life.

He tells a story from the start of the documentary project when he and Mila went to look at coffins. They weren't allowed to film inside a funeral parlour in London, but on a visit back to Bolivia they managed to do it. Amaru laughs as he repeats his conversation with the owner:

"I'd like to look at coffins."

"May I ask who the coffin is for?"

"For me!"

Amaru mimics the owner's expression, which Mila caught on film. I wince at how he plays the joker, making fun of the man's dismay.

Now, Amaru isn't talking about a funeral, and he doesn't want to be buried "down there, under the ground." He imagines his death like launching into space, a rocket man. A craftsman friend back in La Paz has built him a two-metre-high space capsule out of plywood and aluminium: his vehicle "to disappear," which awaits him in the museum.

As Amaru acts out his dreams, I'm remembering the astronomy picture books he loved as a child, the ones he'd fall asleep reading. I'm thinking of planetarium shows and photo exhibitions we've visited together, and my own fascination with the sky at night. Now it's their project, his and Mila's, together in their creative bubble, their Bolivian-English backgrounds mirroring each other, their love stronger than romance. She's been with him all the way, his special friend, his guide through the documentary production.

It's getting late, but the pizza-making has been postponed. Amaru has jumped ahead to an idea for another scene. He's asking me to film him and I'm doubtful I can do it.

"I'm not very good at this... it may come out wobbly."

"Never mind."

He means, I just have to try. Many times, Amaru has offered to teach me how to use his smart TV and digital printer, "for when I'm not here," he says, looking me in the eye.

I've always refused, saying,

"Not now... it gives me a headache. I'll do it another day."

The truth is, I only want to do those things with him. I don't even want to think about doing them on my own. Tonight, there's no-one else to film him, so I'll have to learn it on the spot.

Amaru goes to the kitchen door and puts my backpack on the floor. He pulls out the old wooden chair to use as a prop and hands me his phone. He walks me over to the far end of the kitchen and sets me up facing the chair. Standing behind me, he positions my arms so I hold up the phone horizontally with both hands. All I have to do is stand there, try to keep the phone steady, and watch. He finds the video recorder button and switches it on.

Amaru leaps back to the chair, stands on it, and lifts his arms like a diver about to plunge into an Olympic pool. He bends his knees, jumps, and lands with a loud thud, crouching on the floor in front of the chair. He's bending forward, head in his hands, as if in prayer. I'm shocked, and worried that his knees might be bruised. He gets up and grins—so typical of him, that look—and I switch off the video.

Now I feel dazed, as if I were the one who'd jumped. I glance over at the red Formica clock. "It's half past eleven at night! We must be disturbing the neighbors downstairs."

Amaru shrugs that off with a smile. It really isn't important, and we both know that. The neighbors are friends, and his performance is heroic. In an instant he's by my side with the phone, using his favorite app to edit the video. This is something he's good at, part of a skillset that's remained intact through his illness. He experiments with playing back the film on various speeds. First, he appears tumbling down fast, like an accidental fall. Then he drops in slower motion, floating to the floor. The slowest edit looks the best to me: his jump is purposeful, hands drifting up, his descent gradual, his prayer pose a poem.

How can I cope with my son's enactment of his moment of death? When I filmed Amaru's jump, I heard the thud of his landing and felt its vibration. Now, watching the replay, there's something that won't let me hear that noise. It's as though, by blanking it out, I'm magicking away the time when Amaru will "disappear" for real. I'm connecting with trauma pulsating in and out, storing it within my body, breaking down disassociation, trying to stay conscious in the midst of chaos.

At extreme moments in my life, I've sometimes created memory-pictures and fixated on objects that remind me later that the events were real. An object can make a bridge between an intense experience, detachment from pain, and a return to assurance that the scene really happened. These eyes, now seeing, saw that object then. They see it now. It's the same me, somehow. I can choose to dip in and out of the experience, to take control, unpack it later—or not.

In my early thirties, I had a verbal duel with my mother. Our antagonism had reached a limit that was unbearable for me, and I wanted to free myself from that suffering. I knew I was seeing her for the last time. I fixed my gaze on a glass jar on her bedroom shelf that contained dozens of colored spools of thread. As she spoke, I engraved their image on my mind and thought,

I will never forget this moment.

Now, that jar with its spools lies on its side amidst belongings spread on my livingroom floor, half-packed cases, and bags to take to the charity shop. Will I keep it? Maybe it's already served its purpose.

Now, the object I'm staring at is the chair in the corner near the door. It's from the Victorian era in which this house was built. It has joined hands carved on the back, creaky joints, and a reddish-brown leather seat. I think,

It will never look the same to me again.

It's real to see it empty now. It was real to see Amaru standing on it, jumping off, and crashing to the floor. As I look at the chair, I'm imagining a time when it will hold the void of him no longer being alive. I suddenly catch myself living with the phantom of my son already gone.

At this instant, I start to realise that play-acting and fantasizing are ways Amaru and I both release the terror of separation. Getting close to the reality of dying is healthy for us both. So is celebrating the preciousness of life. I still have time to shake off the delusion that makes future death—his, mine, ours—more present than this flesh-and-blood moment with my son, alive.

It's after midnight, and the Day of the Dead has come and gone. I'm sitting at the table with Amaru in the glow of the red-walled kitchen. We're eating pizza with extra melted cheese and hot black chilli sauce. The filming was a success. Amaru raises a glass:

"Mum, we're free! You and me. No work, no study. We're living the life."

This is what preparing for dying means, before the time of lift-off and the space jump. We welcome the souls as they pass through, making the candles flicker. *Todos Santos* has come and gone, and death is well installed in the room.

SUNDAY

BY SHARON WHITE

It is Sunday, not unlike the Sundays of my childhood but quite unlike the sunny days of my youth when Sundays seemed to drift by in a haze of vagueness and languor.

The sound of raindrops falling on the galvanized roof is home to me. I am sitting in the half-light of my room; the grey glare is subdued by the yellow gauze of my bedroom curtains that lift in little accordion waves with the air from the standing fan. It is a rainy Sunday in December when families are sitting down to long lunches, traditions of rich stews and golden pies. Somewhere in a house alive with the sounds of laughter and relaxed family activity, someone will turn up the radio and turn on the Christmas spirit, and the infectious melody of an *aguinaldo* will waft through the house. On such a Sunday, life in Trinidad is a sensory delight, a luxury blend of colors and flavors so rich, it is heady.

The last time I saw my father alive was on a Sunday. Like so many Sundays before, I was at my parents' house, just them and me.

"Sundays are not the same without the boys," said my mother. "The house came alive... *we* used to come alive."

"Ah, child," my father sighed, "it seems to have weakened us all."

After my divorce, my Sunday visits with my parents became the quiet hours. My father and I would watch the local soap opera on television, and we were often amused by what we saw as versions of ourselves. He and I had shared that spirit ever since our early bike rides through the unpaved roads that cut through the cane fields. As a child, it seemed to me that we rode at fantastic speeds as we snaked through the dirt tracks, whipping up the dry dust and skirting the potholes. I stood on the bar of my father's bicycle in my sturdy little Clarks shoes and felt safe. My father sat behind me, his shoulders protecting me, his eyes alert and watchful to what lay ahead. Years later, though we never spoke of it, I knew that we shared something so solid that nothing, not my frailties or the anxieties I caused, could shake that sense of safety.

That last Sunday, my father and I did not look at the soap opera that hummed unobtrusively in the background. He appeared preoccupied and hesitant, as if he wanted to say something to me. We shifted around each other in the kitchen, and at one point when our eyes met, he turned towards the window. Two days later, I stood over him and watched his body lying in what had been his and my mother's bed for a lifetime. I kissed his face; it was no longer warm, and I wished for just one word more from him. Perhaps what he had wanted to say to me two days earlier was goodbye. Why had I not thrown my arms around him and asked him to tell me or simply hugged him and lingered there? With characteristic humility, he surrendered to the universe, welcoming his last dose of daylight that must have filled him with a brilliance that shocked his heart. It was as if with that one last blow to that organ from which love, and pain, and grief, and joy had spilled year after relentless year, he had said take it, it is full. And with that he smiled and exited this life.

It is evening, and the heavy rain has subsided to a delicate drizzle. I draw the curtains and watch the birds delighting in the dampness. My father's birds always heralded the rain and seemed happiest during a tropical downpour. Maybe just as they could smell the rain they could smell my mother's baking, for that was how she entertained us on rainy days. I recall a childhood that was fragrant with just-baked biscuits and flaky coconut pies; small, yellow *doux douce* mangoes that I would collect in a little plastic bucket as my mother watched from the kitchen; red anthurium lilies clustered in the damp shade of the lime trees; the pungent sweetness of over-ripe fruit that fed the birds. There was a whole world in that backyard of overgrown plants and half-collapsed wire fences. All of this is embedded in my memory, but the smells have remained close to my skin, so close that one rainy Sunday when I'm alone with no parent, no child, no husband, no friend, when I'm too ripe with longing for my familiar loves, the birdsong takes me back to my childhood home where my father is pottering around, and my mother is baking. There was a rhythm to that life that I have tried to capture and reproduce as the essence of what once sustained me. But life has shown me that I need to create my own, and I see now that my children will have to do the same.

Sunday remains a quiet day, a day when if it is raining, I think of those days of insane joy when I splashed around the puddles in my panties only, wishing it would rain forever. At other times, Sunday is like a recycling day for sorting, and discarding, and resolving to make fresh impressions on the dusty tracks that will surely come in the days ahead. I like to think that I would kick and lift the pebbles, that I would stop at times to feel the wind, hear the rustle of the cane leaves, look at their graceful bows, and inhale their sweetness. I am no longer a child perched on the bar of my father's bicycle; I am a woman who drives but who is afraid to try unfamiliar routes. I admired my father's fearlessness, yet I allow fear to restrain me. He was determined to remain present to the joys and travails of life, believing that the measureless, momentary events make up a life, all our lives. A momentary decision to give up or to press on, even on Sunday. So, before the sun begins its descent behind the hills and the quiet gives way to disquiet, I pick myself up and head out to visit my mother. She hasn't called to ask when I'll be coming or to suggest that I put it off because it's getting late. She is no longer conscious of time and the approaching nightfall, which in a very perverse way has released her from her demons.

In the initial stages of the disease, nighttime had become a period of horror for her, a stretch of hours so menacing to her sanity that she went to extreme lengths to conceal the slightest semblance of space between the curtains in her bedroom. Safety pins held the panels together so that no intruder could look in on her as she slept. Later, the panels would mock and terrify her as they became mobile, stalking her with their bizarre, alien shapes.

Now as a sliver of moon emerges from a blanket of cloud, my mother is calm as she is fed and changed into her night clothes. Her eyes stay closed throughout the various homecare rituals, and even as I bend down to kiss her, her eyes are shut. I sit on the edge of her bed and inhale. I so want the smell of her, to capture it and take it away with me, that instinctive, primal, sensory comfort that connects me eternally to her. I put my hand in hers and she takes it so fiercely that I am almost afraid to breathe, for fear that the slightest movement on my part might unsettle her. "Mummy, I'm here," I say to the silence. I tell her about my day and about the boys and make it all sound better than it is, in case she is hearing me.

I look around the room: it is simple, restrained, and functional. I'm searching for signs of my mother. Toiletries are arranged neatly on one side of the dressing table, a small vase of dried flowers on the other, and in the middle counter a jumble of nursing paraphernalia. My mother's life is now contained in this room; there are no books on the bedside table, no rosary, no earrings tossed amidst bits of paper, a note here, a telephone number there, no blouse hanging on the door of the cedar wardrobe. In its place, her next dose of medication sits waiting for the prescribed hour. I want to ask her what she's thinking, what flashes of memory shoot across that tangled brain, whose faces she sees when she closes her eyes, what she dreams about. "Mummy, your hair looks beautiful now that it's silver and no longer rebellious. And your skin! It's just lovely."

I laugh as I ask her if she felt she needed to pass everything on to me, including the facial blemishes she had in her menopause. Her grip remains tight, her tongue silent. Perhaps I could fall asleep lying next to her, her fingers still clutching mine but it's getting late, so I release my hand and let myself go. In the car, I realize that I have brought the scent of my mother with me.

I look over at the passenger seat and picture her sitting there, a feeble, frightened figure folding in on itself. During her last conscious years, my mother did not want to go on. That desire, and the essence of who she was, crumbled with the dirt at my father's grave. I watched, first with panic and then with resentment as she grew inexpressive and indifferent, my mother who had been the source from which my life had sprung, who had nurtured me, whose sensibilities had led me to discover my own.

At my father's funeral, I said to a friend that my mother appeared to be doing surprisingly well.

"The worst is yet to come," he had said. "Have heart."

I don't know which was worse, losing my father or having to watch my mother lose herself. I really did think that she and I would be allies, two women battling an unspeakable loss. Instead, my mother claimed the loss as hers, plunging herself into mourning solitarily and discon-solately. I felt abandoned.

One Sunday, choking with grief, I decided to confront her. "Mummy, you seem to forget that I've lost my father."

"And I have lost a limb," she replied. "I feel as if an arm has been cut off."

The lack of sentiment or self-pity in her voice made me see that her brokenness would not mend. She wore her grief like a shield; she had draped it over herself and had become impenetrable. She shrank, her breasts fell like sad little lumps onto her chest, her collar bone hollow above her skeletal frame. This was grief gone mad I thought; it will wear itself out. No. It wore *her* out, extracted her substance, and left her dry. I was rendered powerless; the forces of love and loss had exerted and exacted themselves. Santimanitay. Sans humanité.

I have been sitting in the car looking at the soft, white rain in the yellow light of the streetlamp outside my mother's window. Her lights have been turned off so it's time for me to go. Maybe tonight the exqui-site notes of "Clair de Lune" will ripple on the shores of her dreams, and she will see a little girl, her long, dark hair in a high ponytail, her bangs low on her forehead. Her daughter is at the piano in a room with soaring ceilings and wooden jalousies. Through the slats, my mother sees my father, his head bent, listening. In that place, with its wide front steps and tall palms standing proud in their bright red pots, my mother is buoyant and free.

DOES ONE TIRE OF ONE'S BEATING HEART?

BY PETER NEWMAN

"That's for sissies," I say, wrinkling my nose.

My mother has just told me I should sing in a choir because a family friend overheard me singing and told her I'm "musical". The snitch who told her, she said, is the "concertmaster" of the Toronto Symphony Orchestra, whatever that means. But I am not a baby, I'm *eight*, and I will *not* be a sissy.

"*Mm-mm*, no," shaking my head.

Mom's eyebrows lift, wrinkling her forehead. "But singing is fun," she says.

No. And that was it for choirs until I turned fifty.

* * *

My earliest memory of my mother is her soft voice singing to me when I was four. The memory morphs into summer mornings five years later. She and I have cleared the breakfast dishes. My father is away at work and my younger sister Jill is in another room, crayoning. The radio is always on "Music in the Morning" while Mom does her housework. It starts each day with a soaring theme from Brahms. As I sweep, helping, its energy flows into my chest, arms.

Around my tenth birthday, my parents take Jill and me to visit the snitch. His name is Elie Spivak, and his wife is Dad's cousin Hilda. Dad drives our 1952 Oldsmobile to their small frame cottage in the country. It is brown with white shutters and looks cozy.

"What's a concertmaster?" I ask. My parents always say the word with awe.

"The leader of the first violins," Mom says. "The most important person in the orchestra."

Hilda serves Jill and me cookies and milk. She is talkative, outgoing, but I am looking at her quiet husband. The concertmaster is short, with thick black eyebrows and black hair combed straight back. He is not laughing like the other grownups.

My father is gregarious. "Elie, could you show your violin to the children?" Dad's blue eyes twinkle. "Maybe even play something for them?"

Mr. Spivak turns to look at me, quiet, dark eyes behind rimless eyeglasses.

He opens his violin case. "This instrument is very special," he says. "It's called a Stradivarius."

He puts it under his chin. "This is for Peter," he says. He looks at me again. "This music is for *you*."

He begins to play, improvising. I have never heard such sounds. They are stirring, forceful. His bow dances, and somehow plays two strings at once, two notes. He plays faster, the music confident and bold. Its energy makes me feel like I could do anything. He has dedicated it to me, and I am given to understand that this is the way he sees me, this powerful man with the special gift. He is telling me that the music is about the kind of boy I will be. I am holding my breath, more than just listening; something is reaching inside me.

* * *

In school that fall, Mom suggests I start the flute in music class. I am allowed to take it home on loan. When I open the case, it is nestled in the blue velvet lining, an amazing intricacy. Myriad keys and levers. Glistening. To reach the farthest keys, I have to stretch as hard as I can with my right little finger until it hurts. When I handle the shiny instrument, I slip into a new and secret realm, taking the pieces out of the case, putting them together; then, after practicing, taking them apart again, carefully placing them into the perfectly fitting hollows of that blue, velvet-lined case.

But I am frustrated by how hard it is to make a sound. Mom gets me a flute teacher. I try to purse my lips the way he shows me, but the silver-plated instrument makes only the sound of my breath— not a note. To show me how, the teacher puts his finger and thumb on each side of my mouth, compressing my lips.

"It's called the embouchure," he says. "For notes to come out, it has to be just right."

"But it's so *hard!*"

"Of course it is." He gestures at Mom's piano, disdainful. "You can walk up to *that* and hit any key with your *nose*, and it will still make the right note." He looks right at me and I am paying attention. "But to know how to make a note on the flute—that's special."

Finally, a first breathy note emerges through the maze of keys, valves, and levers. This is not being a sissy. There is something like a trembling in my arms.

* * *

Three years later, I'm thirteen in a new school and the music teacher has just announced that everybody will be in the band.

"You can choose your instrument," Mr. Rutherford says. He stands in front of the class and demonstrates the snare drum, French horn, clarinet, trombone.

When he comes to the flute it sounds sweet, tender. I also notice it's quiet; other instruments drown it out. Maybe that was okay three years ago. Now, though, my voice is deepening; I am developing body hair and biceps, and this instrument is no longer for me. I need something bold, powerful.

But it suits the prettiest girls in the class, who flock to the flute. As they play, their soft, long hair falls around the instrument. Seeing them creates a strange fluttering in my chest.

Mr. Rutherford opens a rectangular case and holds up a treasure of shiny brass.

"This is a trumpet," he says.

He puts it to his lips, plays a series of thrilling notes. I recognize the rousing theme from "The Lone Ranger". Light glints off the brass.

I shoot my hand up. "I'd like to play that," I say.

I look around; half of the boys in the class have their hands up, like me.

"Wait, we have only five trumpets," he says. But I have put my hand up first and get my wish. It's noble, holding it. I feel like a man, stand taller.

* * *

We are an out-of-tune, ragged bunch. Our parents arrive in the school auditorium for our band performance, looking proud. But as we play, I see my father in the audience shaking silently. He's holding onto his sides to contain himself. I'm petrified he'll lose control, laugh out loud.

The next year we sound more like a proper band. The music is clipped to a lyre on my trumpet, and we practice on the school's football field. It's a trick to play while marching in step, trying to keep the flow of air into my mouthpiece smooth during the up-and-down bouncing.

We blare, and we blat. We are majestic.

I take lessons, work to produce a more rounded tone. I learn to double and triple-tongue the fast notes, join an orchestra. When we play a Haydn symphony, Mom leans forward in the audience.

At seventeen, a counselor at a children's summer camp, I wake up the camp each morning with 'Reveille', the stirring military trumpet call. At dusk, the campers' bedtime, I paddle a canoe out on the still lake to play 'Taps'. Liquid trumpet across the water, reaching children in bed, in their cabins. Counselors tell me it calms their anxious and homesick little campers, helps them fall asleep. *Day is done, gone the sun, from the lake, from the hills...* I wait, let the vibrato echo mournfully around the still lake.

In university, I travel with the Varsity Band to football games in other cities where we march through the streets, wearing handsome caps and long capes in the school colors, blue and white. Virile.

Meanwhile, Mom is playing Beethoven sonatas and teaching me piano. We lean forward side by side on the piano bench. My long fingers, inherited from her, try to imitate hers. Hours of scales and finger exercises before the real music. Bach, Chopin; they lift me from the planet I know.

* * *

Thirty-five years after the marching band, soon after my father died, Mom was feeling very low. More than grieving, she was clinically depressed. We went to piano concerts to help her feel better.

She was in the theatre lobby waiting for me. At ninety-one, she had come alone by subway and bus. "I love my independence," she said. "The only hard part was that high step up into the bus."

I took her hand and we walked to our seats. The pianist played Beethoven's Sonata No. 18. It was in my bones from childhood, Mom laboring over it, producing Beethoven's stirring power, then his exquisite tenderness.

The last movement, the Presto, is meant to describe running horses, she said. In 1920, when she was fourteen, she had an after-school job playing it on the piano at the silent movies.

"I would sit just under the stage in the theatre and look up at the screen. If it was a love scene, I played Chopin. And if it was a Western and the horses were running, I played that movement."

Her eyes shone. The memory of the notes swelled within her, squeezing out her depression until there was no room left for it.

* * *

She lived long enough that I could have the pleasure of caring for her, parenting my parent. The first time I put on her shoes, did up her buttons, cut her toenails for her, a deep, startling happiness filled me, to do for her what she had done for me when I was a child.

In old age, she kept her firm opinions. The most damning criticism she could think of was to describe somebody as "crude". Or—just as insulting—"ordinary". The flip side, her greatest compliment, was "cultivated", or "refined". And in regards to music, "sublime". I came to understand the weight of these words.

For her, the Beethoven sonatas were the peak of human aspiration and expression.

My kids asked me, "Why does Grandma play Beethoven so much?" When I told her that, she smiled.

"Somebody," she said, "once asked Claudio Arrau, 'Don't you get tired of playing Beethoven?'"

I nodded, waiting.

"He answered, 'Does one tire of one's beating heart?'"

* * *

At another concert when she was ninety-five, we heard a piano song by Schubert. She closed her eyes, transfixed. Moved, she rested her head in her hands.

"That song was my favourite," she said when it was over. "I used to nearly swoon when playing it."

"Swoon"—nobody in my generation used that word. Yet I felt the bond between us. There's a rapture I've felt playing in an orchestra, singing in a choir. It's unlike anything else. I took her hand: knobbly knuckles, ancient blue veins. Parchment skin.

The concert ended with a prolonged, standing ovation. It was going to force the performers to play an encore.

"I hope they don't," Mom said. I asked why.

"After that... there *is* nothing else."

We walked slowly to my car, her feathery arm cradled in mine. "Sometimes you wonder what is the point of living," she said, voice soft.

"Then you hear music like this, and you realize that yes, life *is* worth living."

* * *

Eventually Mom did tire of her beating heart; at age 102, it stopped.

I merge my car onto the expressway, sixteen lanes, eight in each direction. Looking ahead, at the side mirrors, rear-view mirror, gauging crazy movement all around me. Cars weave sharply in and out of lanes at 130 kilometers an hour. With the hypervigilance, a tightness grips my throat.

I crave the antidote. I turn on the car radio and a station is playing the theme from "Music in the Morning" that I remember from the childhood summers with my mother. It envelops, surges in my chest. The tension in my throat drains away; I am drenched with music. I am somehow still alert to the complex traffic around me but I feel a lightness now, pulled, like her, out of crudeness into the sublime; singing aloud, loud, feeling the rhythms, lifting. Mending.

Sometimes we search for our beating heart, and sometimes it searches for us.

PILE ON

BY DANA WEBSTER

"Hey, King, how fast you think you can run?" That's twelve-year-old Ronnie Burns calling me by my last name. Behind dark sunglasses, his eyes are hard to read. It's a Saturday afternoon in 1973, late spring and, like pack animals, some of us neighbourhood kids have gathered at the park and plopped ourselves down around the picnic table. I brought my baseball glove in case of a pick-up game.

"I dunno. Pretty fast," I shrug, surprised that a boy in grade 7 would even talk to me, a girl in grade 5. We don't even go to the same school anymore.

"You wanna test that out?" He lifts his sunglasses to his forehead and winks at Jimmy who I don't think even goes to school at all, not since he and Ugly Rob set fire to the Church of the Redeemer last year, and they "went away" for a while.

"Um, sure, I guess." I play along imagining he'll time me as I run the bases at the diamond, a competition we've all played before.

Ronnie flicks his cigarette sideways and says, "Then you better fucking run."

His voice turns cold, no longer playful. I look around the picnic table: Ronnie, his older brother Bob, Jimmy, Woody, Tommy, and Kenny who's carving his initials into the wooden tabletop with a pocketknife. Their eyes shift from one to another, animated, wondering what the game is, hoping they can play, too. Next to me, my best friend, Sarah, fiddles with her braids.

The tone of Ronnie's voice is one I've heard before from boys in my own grade, but this feels different. There are more boys here than usual and except for Tommy who is in my class, they're older. The most boys I'd ever had to fend off at one time was two.

There were only a few of us girls the boys picked on. The ones with boobs like Kerry and Caitlin and even Debbie, before she got pregnant at thirteen last year. I'd watched with everyone else the time Kerry cry-laughed when Woody untied the back of her halter top as she drank from the water fountain, her boobs exposed to all us kids. And when Jimmy stuck his hands up Caitlin's mini skirt, daring someone, anyone, to make him stop while she tried to wriggle free. I hung my head and looked away, grateful that it wasn't me that time. Kerry and Caitlin were easy pickings. Debbie had learned to fight—throw punches and bite. I learned to fight back, too, kicking and swinging my arms wildly, spitting sometimes, or whenever I'd get a head start, I'd run and scream *fuck you*, a phrase my mother would be horrified to know I used in public.

Not that it saved me every time or even half the time. For two years, starting when I was new to the school in grade 3 till now, I've been chased, caught, kissed, punched, groped, and name called. My mother wore herself out insisting I dress like a girl at school with skirts and leotards and buckled shoes. But I refused just as violently. No way was

I going to make it easier for anyone to get at my body parts. I took to wearing my dad's oversized shirts and sweaters, high-waisted jeans, and sneakers with which I could make a fast get-away.

For now, I'm thinking I'll just get up and leave quietly and maybe they'll let me go. There's no one else around. Only the dark, quiet houses that line either side of the park are witness.

I say to Sarah, "I'm going home. You wanna come with me?" as I shift my legs out from under the table. I want her to say yes.

"Didn't I tell you to run?" Ronnie says as he, too, starts to stand up. "Think I'm kidding around?"

So, I start to run, my heels dig into the grass, as I head in the direction of the sidewalk to home. I'm fast. I have long legs. I'm good at track and field, the 20-metre sprint, hurdles, high jump. I kick my legs into high gear. But the distance between the picnic table and the sidewalk feels a million miles away.

The ground behind me vibrates and I know I'm being chased. "Gotcha," Ronnie hollers as his hands push me from behind. I lose my footing and stumble. His arms wrap around my waist in a football tackle, and the weight of him lands on top of me. The wind is knocked out of me as my face hits the hard, grassy playing field.

I've landed on my stomach. "Turn her over. Turn her over," I hear. Hands are upon me. I know if they turn me over, all is lost. I thrash my body, side to side, my arms tucked tightly to my sides. I yell, "Stop it, fuck, stop it." They're too strong for me, there are too many of them.

I can't breathe, I can't move. My arms and legs are pinned to the ground, my shoulder digs into the earth. The weight of them crushes me. Hands are down my pants and up my shirt grasping, pinching, groping. Rank tobacco breath chokes the tiny air pocket I have. Half-chewed fingernails scrape deeply across my belly and tender breasts. I pull my legs closed as best I can but then a finger roughly shoves its way inside me. I gasp with the sharp pain and buck my hips hoping to dislodge it.

"I got it!" someone whoops in triumph.

I want to keep fighting. I should keep fighting but I have lost the will. The worst is done. I open my eyes and see that beyond the heads of dirty-haired boys, beyond the smell of the thrashed earth beneath me, there is a blue sky and cottony white clouds that I can nestle myself into and wait it out.

When I stop resisting, the onslaught stops, too. One by one, they get off me. A couple of them give my head an extra push into the ground. Hands slap together. Someone says, "What a slut." I lay for a moment just trying to breathe. I'm crying; I can't help it and I hate myself for it. I pull my knees to my chest and place my hands over my throbbing breasts, hating them, too, for just being there.

I push myself to sitting, pull down my t-shirt and adjust my pants. *Stop crying, you stupid baby*, I scold myself. I wipe the back of my hand across my nose. Mixed with snot is blood, which I wipe on the grass. I search for the clouds from before but they have re-formed and drifted away. I feel a determination, an angry and vengeful spirit rise up in me. The scorch of the afternoon sun burns my bare arms.

I stand up on shaky legs and move in the direction home. I can hear the low chatter of the boys back at the picnic table and smell the smoke of their cigarettes.

"There she goes," says Ronnie. "Hey, King, not so fast after all, eh?"

"Fuck you," I scream back. And they laugh like they're already bored.

My beloved wide-bottomed GWG Scrubbies are streaked with grass stains. A bit of damp mud and small tufts of grass ripped from their roots are smashed into the knees. I wipe them off as best I can.

"Dana, wait up." It's Sarah. I can tell she's running to catch up, but I keep walking. "Dana," she tries again. Out of breath, she reaches my side and slows down to my pace.

After a few seconds, she asks, "You going home?" She hands me my baseball glove.

"Yeah," I say. "Thanks."

"Ronnie's such a jerk. Don't let him get to you," she says, like she knows anything about it. She doesn't have boobs yet; no one ever even notices her. "I tried to make them stop ..."

"Yeah, whatever. I don't care." I tell myself that every time this happens to me.

But I don't believe it. Revenge fantasies run through my mind, like me knocking on Ronnie Burns's house and telling his mother what he did. Or maybe I'd sneak up behind Tommy and kick the back of his knees, so he'd fall over in front of everybody.

Sarah takes my hand, and it calms me a little. "I hate that fucking Ronnie Burns," I say, still shaking with rage.

We walk to the end of the street in silence. At Yonge Street, we pause. Sarah lives two blocks south and my house is two blocks north.

"You wanna get popsicles later?" she asks.

"Maybe," I say. "I'll call you later."

When I reach home, my mother is in the backyard deadheading her geraniums. An open pack of Belmonts and a pale-yellow lighter sit on the umbrella table. A half-smoked cigarette hangs from her lips as she bends over the potted flowers.

"Hey, Mom," I say, casually, before she looks up. I'm hoping my voice carries no tone, nothing that suggests anything is out of the ordinary. I make to open the screen door but am stopped.

"What's that on your jeans?" She peels the cigarette off her lips and stares at me through her Hollywood starlet sunglasses.

"Just some grass." I make a show of brushing the debris away, allowing for a pause to see if this time she'll notice my shaking hands, the tears riding close to the surface. I haven't always come home looking like this after an assault. Most of the time there were no outward signs, but I'd thought that because she's my mother, she'd see my invisible wounds anyway. This time, the evidence was clear and yet she looked right past me into the distance to a place I imagine she sees where her daughter doesn't come home beaten up and sullen, where mothering was effortless and devoid of complications, where she can just smoke cigarettes and drink coffee.

"You're too hard on your clothes," she says. "Hang on, what about your t-shirt? Is it ripped?" She comes closer, the cigarette smoldering between her fingers, the sun glinting off her deep red nail polish. With her thumb and last two fingers, she takes hold of the orange *Neil Diamond* shirt my brother gave me for my birthday and pulls the material toward her. The smoke runs up my nose and I look away.

"Jesus, Dana," she shakes her head, poking one long red nail through a hole. "Go on in and get cleaned up. Don't forget to set the table for dinner."

* * *

I didn't forget.

A LONGING

BY BARCLAY MARTIN

At Baba's funeral, I am the last one to kiss her cheek. Her skin is cool and hard, framed by creamy roses and a black fur stole. On her feet are a pair of sparkling gold slippers. It is late spring when we bury my grandmother, the ground trying to thaw under the bite of a receding winter wind. A black and yellow tractor is stationed next to the gravesite, and the fresh earth edged with frost sits in a mound beside its steel jaws.

At Baba's deathbed I wanted to wet her dry lips with the moisture from a folded towel sitting beside me. Instead, I held her reluctant hand, motionless at her side, and extended my other arm across her body to hold my mother's hand. When Baba left us, a sound drew out from my mother's mouth surprising us all, *Mommy*. I had never heard her call to Baba with such affection or such longing. *Mommy* held everything she would never let herself say, and everything Baba could never hear.

Cars whip past me on Jasper Avenue as I wait for the light to change. I can see the shadow of my great aunt's building ahead, reflected between clouds on the tall glass of a high-rise. I make my way across the street and down the long block to the entrance of the nursing home. Salt and gravel crack under my boots like broken glass.

I haven't seen Auntie Rosie in twenty years, not since the details of a painful secret had come back to Baba's door wrapped in other people's voices. Rosie and Baba used to live in the same apartment building and would swap recipes spiced with sisterly gossip, take turns hosting family for the holidays, and carry on our small traditions as red embroidered dishware filled the table with the sweet smell of bread.

At the wide doors of the building, I can see the shimmers of staff carrying trays and folks waiting in wheelchairs. I hesitate, wondering if somehow Baba knows I'm stepping across enemy lines. Wind nips at the soft skin of my ankles and urges me inside.

At the reception I ask directions to Rosie's room. The nurse cocks his eyebrow. "She's never mentioned you before." Electricity runs up the nape of my neck and purrs, *intruder*. I look over my shoulder for the exit, but the nurse has already walked me to the elevator, and I am being pulled up towards her.

Rosie's door is open, and I find her in an armchair by the window. I kneel on the carpet next to her, and gently take her hand.

"Whose daughter?" She squints at me through large gold-rimmed glasses. Her curled hair is the same muted brown I remember, and I squint back to see if her roots are showing. My fingers tremble in her hand.

Holding my Baba's hand always had a time limit. I would clutch at her dangling fingers with both hands and slide against the smooth polyester of her handmade pantsuit as we wove our way through the Kingsway

Mall and into the belly of the fabric store. I would watch in awe as she flipped neatly through soft paper envelopes with drawings of thin white women modeling the latest fashions. At home in the afternoon, women with thick curves and thicker accents would gather in Baba's sewing room for their fittings, leaving behind their perfume and empty teacups swirling with whispers of the Old Country.

Other mornings, Baba and I would scour the bright wide aisles of discount markets with handfuls of coupons, searching for tart shells and malt ice cream. I would smile up at Baba, my lips wet with grease as she fed me slices of kolbassa at the deli counter before heading home. All the time, running for her hand.

Rosie decides the laundry must be tended to, so I haul her up from the sofa and she gathers a couple of items into a basket. I wonder if she wants to see that I exist outside the walls of her room, wants to make sure I'm not an apparition who has finally come to haunt her. I pick up the basket and we walk down the hall.

I put her clothes in the washer and the metal door slams shut. She supports herself against my body as we weave back down the hallway to her room and fall together onto the chesterfield. The couch has a cream and maroon floral pattern, and I am surprised to notice that it's no longer covered in plastic.

The last time I remember Rosie was in her apartment packed with cousins at Christmas. My mother and I entered quietly and managed to squeeze behind the kitchen table so that we had a physical barrier between us and The Relatives. My mother ate white bread and grew flowers instead of vegetables. My mother married and divorced a Protestant but proudly kept his last name, a name she had earned. We had sat on the floor at the end of the plastic-wrapped chesterfield, tucked between the arm of the couch and a side table with a brimming ashtray. The room was awash in red and gold, an icon of Jesus and Mary sat in the corner with a handful of gathered wheat. My knees were bony under my chin, and a bowl of food was on the shag carpet at my feet. I was still a child, and small enough that people bent over to speak to me, supporting their hands on their knees.

"Whose daughter?" Rosie asks again and we sink gently into the dementia dance. Eventually something sticks and I become Baba's daughter, which feels close enough.

"We had eight, ten cows, us older girls milked them. If you wanted to go to town, Mom and Dad would hitch up the horse to a buggy." Rosie pauses but her eyes are sparkling as her memory spools out. "Vicky was the baby. We'd wrap her up and take her to the fields. Row by row we worked—picked her up and put her down."

I look around the room and find myself categorizing her things, comparing them to the memories of Baba's home. Wondering what is old, what is new, what's hiding in the cupboards. A ceramic tooth-pick jar with red embroidery. A small doll with brown hair dressed in ribbons. A fridge magnet with a blue and yellow flag. Embroidered pansies and crosses in round wooden frames. I want to ask Rosie about every object, and despite myself, I want something from her.

Baba has been gone thirteen years. I search the edges of Rosie's eyes and mouth for echoes of her sister. I listen for her in the timbre of Rosie's voice. I wonder where Baba's ghost is in the room, if she's holding guard at the doorway or shaking her head beside me, arms crossed against her belly.

I want Rosie to bring me my Baba. I want her to pull off her brown wig and *be* my Baba. I want to take her hand to see if her fingertips are still glossy like a pearl from being a seamstress. I want her to offer me krustyky and kolbassa so I can lick sugar and grease off my lips, and eat and eat and eat, just to make her happy.

We go into her bedroom looking for photos when Rosie opens a drawer and shows me a shawl that belonged to her grandmother, Mosha. Black fringe drips from the edges, giving stems to the embroidered roses.

"She wore it like this," and Rosie wraps the shawl over her head, tucking the corners tight under her chin, pushing her cheeks up into her glasses. I remember an old photo with Mosha in front of a clapboard house, her features dark gouges in her square face.

"I don't know who would want this," Rosie says, and it slides from her shoulders like water.

I want to reel the words back into my mouth, but they are already on their way towards her: "I can keep it for you?"

Rosie looks at me from the corner of her eye and shakes her head.

I feel a shame burning in my chest, Baba's anger behind me. How dare I ask Rosie for anything. The drawer shuts with a pop of air and seals our words inside.

Rosie walks me to the elevator. As I enter the small room and turn my back, she calls me sweetie. I look up at her and she says it again, drawing it out like a song. Framed by the closed doors of her neighbor's rooms, she looks small and far away. The black gaps in the elevator threshold become an abyss we can no longer cross. She reaches towards me as the doors clatter, gaining speed. I lift my hand and wonder what we are both reaching for.

The early evening is darkening at the edges as I step outside. I look into the wide moving sky, my ears loud with silence of falling snow.

A CHICKEN'S LAUGH

BY MARTHA MORRISON

"She laughed like a chicken who just laid an egg," my grandma used to say, an old country expression from her girlhood on the farm. It's been two years since I left Toronto to marry a farmer and move to the rural area in southwestern Ontario where my grandma grew up. I'm still stumbling through this foreign bucolic world with sayings I don't understand and chickens I've only recently learned not to fear.

I take a deep breath, pull my shoulders back to show I'm not afraid, and walk into the hen house to collect the day's eggs. Rose, one of our red hens, is still perched in the laying box. She looks at me with that chicken expression that I project my human emotions onto. A chicken's face never looks quite happy, but I'm certain today she looks bothered by my interruption.

The dog pants behind me, his breath warm on my bare leg. I'm sure he's hoping today might be the day that he's finally granted passage into the chicken coop, but I nudge him away with my foot without taking my eyes off Rose. Truthfully, I don't know that it's Rose. All the hens look alike to me, but I can tell them apart by their eggs. One lays small, speckled eggs—I attribute those to Chickie. Another lays dark brown eggs, which I decide belong to Penny. But Rose lays my favourite eggs—extra-large, misshapen, delicious.

Then it happens. In my two years of being a chicken owner, I've never caught this moment. Rose (I assume) lowers her head and ruffles her feathers, raising her rear end high in the air, she squeezes a few times and then *plop* lays an egg right in front of me. *Bock bock bock bock!* She laughs with pride. She laughed like a chicken who just laid an egg.

I can't help but join in her glee, wanting to burst into applause for her accomplishment. "I feel you, Rose!" I say, thinking of my own fertility journey. The strips that let me know when I'm ovulating, laying an egg as it were. "Honey, I'm ovulating!" *Bock bock bock bock!*

Rose looks at me. This time, a blank stare. Another canvas for my projections. "Ec-top-ic," the doctor had said after I'd tripped over the word for the second time. An egg in the wrong spot.

Sometimes a hen will lay an egg in the wrong spot, while she's out foraging in the yard instead of in the hen house. The egg gets pecked at or crushed or swiped by the dog. It never survives. One hen wouldn't give up and abandon the egg she laid out in the field, no matter how I tried to coax her back into the safety of the hen house. It still didn't survive. And she didn't either.

The ectopic pregnancy is not viable. An egg doesn't survive in the wrong spot. "If the miscarriage doesn't complete on its own, it will have to be terminated," the doctor says. That's what they call an abortion at the fertility clinic.

An abortion. I used to say I was "pro-choice, but I would never do that" until a friend, who had been through the procedure after a date rape, told me that was a shitty, sanctimonious thing to say. Now I understand. As if the daily news headlines are conspiring against my internal struggle like some internet age version of pathetic fallacy, the possibility of Roe v. Wade overturning in the United States dominates the news and, suddenly, everyone is an expert on reproductive health. Even that word 'ectopic' makes its way into the daily lexicon as lines are blurred as to whether or not women would still receive the lifesaving care they need in these situations. I make a mental note to name the next pair of roosters I'm forced to separate Roe and Wade.

The doctor wants to avoid this procedure. The drugs required might interfere with my ovulation for three to six months, impeding our ability to try again. I do the math. I'm thirty-nine years old and, even though I have a son, I long to give him a sibling. Three to six months of no eggs is not good.

The miscarriage 'completes' in a pool of blood on the bathroom floor the next day followed by a trip to the emergency room for a dilation and curettage. A month later, I'm cleared, at least physically, to try again. The male fifty-something doctor acknowledges that after what I've been through, I may not feel emotionally ready. "But time is not on your side," he adds, as if I've never had that thought. My husband is ten years older than me, yet not once has he been told that time is not on *his* side.

The miscarriage makes me feel rejected, like a woman spurned. *You were inside me and now you're not.* It doesn't make sense, I know. But these situations exist in a dimension that supersedes logic. I bury what I can of the baby-that-almost-was and whisper a name over the gravesite. A butterfly floats by. In the weeks that follow, I eat almost nothing, as if I don't deserve even an ounce of the baby weight I put on in my excitement.

Rose jumps off her perch, interrupting my thoughts, and scurries out of the hen house to the yard with the other chickens, pecking away at the clover. I collect the warm egg. It is extra-large and misshapen with a ridge running along one side. So, it was Rose.

Inside the farmhouse, I crack the egg above the hot, oily pan. I've never eaten an egg this fresh, and my hunger grows as I scramble the orange yolk together with fresh cream for breakfast, throwing a few bits to the dog, my loyal companion. When I'm finished, I take an ovulation test. It's time. We can try again. And somehow, I know that laughter will return to my life. Like a chicken who's just laid an egg.

WHEN I RAN FROM NOTHING

BY CHERYL SUMA

I slip in to watch her last moments of sleep before morning's rise. Sinking into the chair by the window, I'm caressed by the shadows. We are familiar, these shadows of the past and I.

I watch as she twitches her dream dance. I am as much short and aching as she is all limbs, long and lithe, tangled amongst the blankets. I exhale as she settles, her dream torture forgotten. In this moment, we are both safe, and I can breathe.

* * *

I've watched as my desire to protect has become too heavy for her to carry—an unintended burden instead of a gift. From the moment she was born, I wanted to be her guardian against life's worst offerings. She was an angel well fallen. It was my duty to shield her from the evil that lurked just around the bend. As she grew, however, I came to fear that the world would not have it, that it would instead push all my failings upon us both. I saw how we were at once the same, yet not. How she was still the little me, the girl before the bad things happened. I would do anything to stop these things from happening to her.

So, I keep trying to craft a worthy shield with those splinters of me.

* * *

I shift in my perch. The morning sun has begun to caress her face, taunting me with the reminder that, at least for now, she glows the kind of beauty born from kindness, empathy, and trust.

The bad ones, they'll want to crush that. They'll try to wrest her uniqueness from her or want to claim it as their own. To paint her with their blackness until their hunger dims her light. My thoughts hide behind dramatic lines. I know better. There is just one fear that summarizes all the others—that they will take from her what is not offered willingly and destroy her in the process.

I want to see her soar, to share her heart's joy. Yet fear and my history won't cease screaming at me to stop the world from touching her, from breaking her and taking away her beautiful wholeness.

I abandon the chair's haven to glide out of the room before she wakes. I do not want her to see the fears I exhale as the sun rises.

* * *

My two earliest memories of the perils of male attention both occurred the year I turned five.

The first time, the two boys who lived next door, ages seven and nine, came over to play. They brought this huge butterfly net, one big enough to engulf most of my upper body. They told me to run.

"We'll chase you."

So, I ran, chubby child legs pumping, hair streaming, arms flung wide, screaming and laughing all around the front yard. I remember the fall leaves floating like shattered rainbows all around me while my two friends' warm laughter did what the fall sun couldn't. It was a feeling like no other: the joyous oblivion of the chase, the pure warm love of being.

Pursued, yet safe.

That same fall, I started kindergarten. A few weeks in, my teacher sent me and another classmate, Laura, down to the art room to fetch some paint. For us, the school was still a maze of never-ending halls. On the way back, we took a wrong turn and came upon a janitor. He was heavyset, with that tired look adults get when they've stopped caring.

"Girls, what's that you've got?"

He stepped forward until he filled the hallway. Laura obligingly held up her paint cans. I didn't like his smile and dropped mine, spilling bright yellow paint all over the hall floor. He opened the janitorial closet, then pushed us inside. I grabbed Laura's hand.

"Now we need to clean that up. You're good girls. You'll help."

Run! the survivor inside me said. I looked at Laura's face, but she just nodded and put down her cans.

"You've got paint on your shirt." He started tugging Laura's jumper over her head. I pulled her sideways, back towards the door. His face turned in. "Now, hold on."

His plans were interrupted by the entrance of a young teacher, whose eyes widened as he surveyed the scene. "Didn't realize anyone was in here. Just grabbing paper towels; one of my students is sick." The teacher looked between the janitor and us, then frowned. He stood taller.

"Girls, shouldn't you be in class?"

I didn't need any encouragement. I dragged Laura out the door, our paint forgotten.

* * *

"Mom? Are you up? I'm heading out for my run. Back in sixty!"

Leaving the janitor flashback behind, I track my daughter's progress as she laps the block eight times. I only feel the air enter my lungs on those breaths that coincide with her passage by—the rest of the time, I suffocate.

The first time I was attacked, I was walking alone through the nice family neighborhood where I'd rented a basement apartment, just ten minutes from campus. I felt safe then too. I think I've told her the story one too many times. She always has her answer ready. It triggers a bundle of shame and guilt-tainted emotions. She is correct in much of her response—we do have fewer bushes on our street, it is daytime, not evening, and she knows to watch. She tells me she will be fine.

Nine. She is on her last lap. I force myself to move to the kitchen to begin emptying the dishwasher—so she won't see my frightened face at the window. I punish the dishes. I knock cupboards shut with satisfying thuds. *How not to suffocate her light with my desperate, shielding embrace?* I ache to let her shine and embrace the many rather than only protect her from the dangers of the few.

Yet, for me, it was the few that always found me. Even left behind in the past, banished by my new, carefully controlled existence, I know they exist. Their threat remains alive, somewhere—somewhere my daughter might be, somewhere I might miss if I stop watching.

* * *

I've never told my daughter the full details of the first assault. Or the second, the third, or all the close calls in-between, for that matter. The particulars seem too punishing; they would reconstruct us. I don't want her to look at me differently, to see broken things where she once saw strength and purpose.

I've always felt as though my existence is a mirage; the truth is more akin to that of three fragmented people cobbled together to make one whole. The little girl before; the young woman, positive and assured; and finally, the woman she became after the assaults—fearful and guarded, forever caught in a loop driven by the need to control risk. The three of us are wrapped up in one terrified bundle, just trying to survive, pretending to be strong. Sexual assault/abuse does that—it creates broken survivors, hiding behind shields too heavy to carry alone. I recognize my demons; I've read enough. The abuse stays with you, impacting your relationships and ability to trust. I understand that these experiences drive my reactions to intimacy and have irreparably changed who I could have become without them. Unable to forget the past, I instead attempt to leave these experiences behind by focusing on ways to avoid the chance of it all—by finding ways to keep my daughter safe. To ensure history does not unearth the opportunity to repeat itself.

* * *

My first time was tragically unoriginal, terrifying, and buried me whole in ways I didn't fully understand until it happened again almost a decade later. The first sexual assault occurred after ending a short-term relationship. At the time, the term "date rape" was foreign to me. It was not something our mothers spoke about when I was growing up in the '70s and '80s. When I found myself in a similar situation ten years later, while I now knew the term, I couldn't believe I'd misjudged another man's character for the second time. In each instance, I fought, matching my assailant's determination with my own. Each time, guilt and self-doubt washed through me as I struggled. How did I get here? What mistake did I make? What clue had I missed? How had I not sensed what was to come? Keenly aware of society's tendency to victim-blame, I remained silent, swearing my one confidant and friend aware of the incidents to secrecy. It would take twenty years of healing, learning, and raising a daughter of my own before I could even consider sharing that burden with anyone else.

* * *

Each day, I tell myself that I have left the harm of these assaults in the past. I carefully bundle their memories into the invisible bag I drag behind me. Despite their weight, I lie to myself and say I have healed. I review evidence that I have moved on and found my power (my successful business, my lovely children, the two instances when I spoke up, supporting friends to leave harmful relationships). Yet even when I succeed in pushing the memories away, their stain remains. They haunt my dreams at night; they color my visions for my daughter's future by day. When alone in my bed, I cry their secrets. Invisible tears for invisible scars. For things hiding close in the past—things that cannot be changed.

Too often, I'm awakened abruptly in the dark—by my churning stomach or my pounding heart, which beats in rhythm with my racing thoughts. Tangled nightmare fears of past assaults that manage to dance their way from dreams into consciousness with ease each night. I want to neglect these scars of the past, to truly leave them behind for good, but they are thick and stubborn and demand my attention.

Panic, even that triggered by events left in the past, is harder to resist once the light fades.

* * *

Not all my dreams are nightmares. Some nights, I dream of my daughter and me—both small, both whole. Beautiful little girls holding hands with our too-thick hair flowing behind us, laughing and running as I used to run.

When I ran from nothing. Pursued, yet safe.

If only it could be that way. For all women, everywhere. Sadly, some dreams can take lifetimes to chase. Perhaps, I've had my fair share of dreams fulfilled already. I count my blessings.

Still, I relish those happy before-fantasies of the two of us. In those dreams, we are spirit twins—unscathed and innocent, always hopeful. Still untouched, we are unafraid to live. We do not yet know that our enemies exist.

In our blessed ignorance, we run because we can, not because we must.

WHERE SKIN BEGINS

BY JULIA CAMPOS

I remember her skin first. It was very pale, sprinkled with gold and brown dots: nameless constellations on a milky canvass. It was very similar to mine. In a way, it continued me. Except that where my skin was smooth and bouncy, hers was paper-thin, threatened by the lightest scratch. My grandmother was covered in minuscule mountains and valleys where time had played without forgiveness.

Ilda was her name. Maria Ilda Campos, paternal grandmother. She was the one who cared for me most weekends, when my very young mother tried to be free, and my father tried to be.

Although she died over a decade ago, I only recently found my grandmother's absence within me. It wasn't so much her death that I grieved then, but the memory of her, the missing story that would unite her yesterday and my present, that would sew our fabrics together.

I knew that she was of Portuguese descent, due to the ubiquitous presence of the Rooster of Barcelos in her apartment—pillows, towels, plates, magnets—and because my father often joked about her alleged moustache. She had been adopted at a very young age. That was all I had of the story that was also mine.

Many months ago, I was translating a novel in which the main character had to say goodbye to a grandfather who raised her, and it struck me violently that I never knew the names of my grandmother's parents. There was a large missing stretch on this skin that I shared with her, a mysterious part of my identity whose aching absence I had never been able to pinpoint. So, I set out to find it.

* * *

The rocking chair is uncomfortable. The dark wood pokes at our backs despite the brown pillow with an embroidered rooster that sits there, in an attempted invitation. The chair belongs to my stern and silent grandfather. After he dies, leaving no tears behind, no one else will sit there. The chair will die with its main occupant.

I look at Vovó Ilda's cold white hands wrinkled by age, holding my small body. I see the milk in the bottle rocking back and forth in tandem with the chair. In these moments that will settle like dust as my very first memories, everything stops so she can tend to me. It is written somewhere that every child must be someone's miracle. I am hers.

With my head leaned back in the dark living room, I see the painting on the wall upside down: cloaked men and a frail dog try to make their way through a snowstorm, as if attempting to escape the frame. It is a painful journey, but I remain indifferent to suffering in the arms of the woman who rocks me.

Years later, I will see the painting in my mind's eye and taste milk in my mouth. A taste of dust and old love. I will never find that painting again. Perhaps it will join my grandfather and his rocking chair in the dark mansion of things that vanish before we love them.

Unlike the chair, the grandfather, and the painting, my grandmother already inhabits me when she leaves this world. She has left a mark, not unlike the scars I have, on which I can't quite locate pain. I wish I had been able to keep her wedding dress, her scarves, or her story, but I got instead the paleness of her skin, the roundness of her edges, and the nameless constellations of her freckles.

* * *

I was able to find the names of my great-grandparents on the internet: Emília dos Santos and Belarmino Andrada. It struck me that my grand-mother's maiden name, Maria Ilda dos Santos, carried her mother's surname, not her father's. I wondered what kind of wreckage Belarmino had caused to inspire this choice and was reminded that I erased my own father when naming my children. Could history repeat itself, I wondered, even when it isn't passed down through narrative? Could my skin remember a story that I had not lived?

* * *

The apartment is unusually dark for noon on a sunny Saturday. The blinds are closed. My sister and I have been lost in the fragile world of child play. I am six years old. She is eight. From her superior position as the eldest, she knows what to do when the storm begins.

She pulls me by the hand, and we find ourselves suddenly huddled together in a very small closet used to keep vinyl records. The closet is old and smells like it. I'm not sure whether it is my heartbeat that I feel or hers, my panting breath or hers that I inhale. My skin feels cold and clammy with fear. From in there we hear the thunder outside: the unfiltered yelling of the small man we both call father, though only I share his genes. The yelling is directed at his mother, my white and ample grandma, who—I can see through the slits on the wooden door—sits quietly, her head lowered at the table, avoiding the objects that zoom by. She seems to have turned out the lights inside, hoping that the hurricane will notice her absence and move on. The storm isn't altogether new. We've experienced it many times, but occasionally, like today, there is an edge to it, a threat of excess that no one wants to see accomplished.

When the apocalyptic silence falls, we come out of the closet with aching throats from contained tears and I watch my grandmother pick up the pieces of my favorite crystal glass. I look into her eyes to see if she has made it back. Her fingertip bleeds and in the redness of her blood I realize that she has been there all along.

* * *

I didn't know what I was looking for in the process of hunting down her story. I felt as though the quilt of our shared skin was torn and in need of sutures. I mended the gaps in a trance-like state experienced only by those who find doors to secret universes. I spent hours imagining the life of a great-grandmother whose name I had only recently learned: Emília.

Overwhelmed by my own curiosity, I got in touch with my estranged father to ask about what the internet couldn't answer. He helped me to fill in the blanks. I found that Emília had three children (I never knew my grandmother had siblings) and eventually disappeared. It was said in the family that she had moved to a convent in France, but my father doesn't seem to think this is true. Emília was never mentioned, she had become something of a taboo. She is also the only family member for whom I haven't been able to locate any identification documents.

* * *

There is a vaguely familiar body on the narrow hospital bed. The light is harsh and white, keeping any bold sweetness from entering the aseptic room. On the wall, a child's drawings—color and innocence—disrupt all the useful and unpleasant things around them. On the bed, they tell me, is a living body; but a machine oversees its breathing, rising and lowering a chest that no longer seems inhabited by soul. I feel that I should touch her hand, but I can hardly recognize it as one. The swollen skin seems to have swallowed her wedding ring. Her familiar paleness has been replaced by a greyish yellow that repulses me. In my chest there is a gaping hole where I cannot touch bottom. As much as I try, I can't reach.

My grandmother is in a coma. I am here to say goodbye. I haven't seen her in nearly a year (I live abroad now), and I can't recall the last time I felt the touch of her skin. Because I can't find the joy, the vivacity, or the warmth with which she always welcomed me, and because I was never taught to chat with death, I don't find a recipient for my goodbye. I cage the animal that tries to rip through my chest and manage two words: oi, vó.

Hi, grandma.

Closed until then like the coffin that awaits them, her eyes suddenly blink repeatedly, and I feel afraid. I realize that the seemingly empty shell in front of me still harbors something inside it that recognizes my voice. But the animal escapes my grip and I unlearn my words. I stand there in silence and watch the blurry image of her life slip away.

* * *

It was a thread that I couldn't stop chasing. I dreamed of going to Vila da Ponte, where my great-grandparents were born, and finding out more about my origins. In every bit of information I uncovered, I found another piece of a grandmother whom I loved dearly, but who deprived me of her rich, complex, and often tragic story.

In this patchwork quilt of skin that I mended chaotically, I discovered holes whose echoes I had felt on my body for a long time. They were ripples of absence, of secrets and stories untold. It was my own skin that I mended, but my ancestors' wounds that I healed. I didn't know where my grandmother was buried, but I could locate the bridge that gave her parents' village its name, *Vila da Ponte*. I could look at pictures of this medieval bridge and wonder if that was where Emília and Belarmino had met, if that was where my skin began.

* * *

I am in her apartment, aware that this is a dream. She stands in front of me and because I know of the impossibility of what I see, I take it in, I touch her skin, I inhale her presence. We sit down on the beige couch, and I ask her all the questions. Because we are in my wishful world, she answers without hesitation, holding my hand. She retreats to her room for a nap, and I am left alone in this space that exists only in my memory. I look closely at the many trinkets on the wooden furniture and feel their dust on my fingertips. I pocket a few in hopes that they will cross realms with me. I don't have much time left. I hold on to my senses, attempting to make it last longer. Warm tears cover my cheeks, it's time to go. I leave quietly (I don't want to disturb her sleep). I close the front door, vibrantly aware that it only opens from the inside. I never owned a key. As I make my way towards the building's exit, I notice the elevator. My grandmother lives on the ground floor, at street level: there is no need for me to take it. But something in it calls to me, so I open the elevator door. In the exposed gears, something shiny draws my eye. In fact, there are several small, twinkling objects all around. I crouch down and pick them all up, one by one. I have found the misplaced pairs of my very favorite earrings. Their lonely, useless partners have been in a box for years, teeming with nostalgia and hope. My subconscious likes metaphors: the memories I leave in this building are some of my most precious treasures.

* * *

Throughout the last year, I have found that revisiting difficult memories is like picking at a scab. If you do it too soon, the soft crust will cling to the wounded skin, stinging and bleeding. You will be undoing the progress, forcing the skin to begin its healing anew. If you give it time, however, the crust will become dry, rugged, thick, and dark brown like the bark of a tree. When you peel it off, instead of blood you will find reinvented, fresh skin. Without any conscious input from you, time performs an invisible magic: the silent regeneration of something that once ached. Something that is now reborn.

MEMORY, ETERNAL

BY IOANNA SAHAS MARTIN

It's raining; a hard, driving rain that pounds on the roof, reverberating on the metal shingles. On the veranda, a hammock swings with the wind. A dog barks in the distance. Banana and palm trees in the ravine wave and flutter as the rain water rushes down the street, quick like a river. Inside the house a fan turns, creaking with each rotation as a line of tiny ants makes its way along the counter towards, or away from, an unseen crumb. Photos on the fridge, on the shelves: of my children, of my aunt's wedding, of my mother and her sisters, of my cousins as children, of my grandfather; some fraying at the corners and yellowing with time, others in small metal frames rusting in the humidity.

When I arrived on the island a week ago, my aunt picked me up at the airport. It was night, the outline of the island visible from the air as the plane came in for a landing, a sprinkle of lights against the darkness of the sea around it. As soon as we got to the house she informed Abuela that we were going to the beach house. She preferred to drive at night. Cooler, quieter. Abuela didn't want to go. *No, no, no. No me voy*—I'm not going. She refused to budge, refused to be manipulated, coaxed, coerced or tricked into going anywhere.

I laughed, glad to see her defiance despite her age and frailty. I moved to lead her down the stairs to the waiting car on the driveway. She dug her fingernails into my arm in protest. *No. No me voy!* She shouted, but it came out only as a hoarse whisper, her vocal chords having been severed in a botched surgery years before. She hung onto the railing and would not budge. Then, as if to taunt us, she sat on a chair in the middle of the veranda, swung one leg over the side and began to pick her fingernails.

For one whole hour she refused us, ignored our pleas, shook her head: *No me voy*. We were impotent in the face of her will. She had 92 years of practice and all the time in the world. Then, finally: *Voy al baño*. After going to the bathroom, she acquiesced, without a word of explanation and allowed me to lead her to the car. We finally drove away at midnight. We stopped at a gas station for a pee break and she beamed at the attendant—happy, peaceful.

I awoke the next morning to the sound of roosters, everyone else still sleeping. I took my journal and stepped out onto the patio. It was cool outside, after the morning rain. Everything smelled fresh and clean, the hills before me pregnant with tropical vegetation. In the distance: the sound of Coast Guard helicopters looking for migrants; the sun rising behind the mountain, warm rays resting on my white limbs. Chickens hobbled across the neighbour's yard, and roosters crowed even though it was long past dawn. An empty hammock swayed in the wind. I allowed myself to sink into it, surrounded by bougainvillea and hibiscus, palm trees, the salty smell of the sea on the wind.

We spend the days poolside, with margaritas and magazines. Green geckos chase each other on the electric wire. They walk delicately, with no fear of falling, and stop in frozen animation as soon as they feel my stare, fully aware of my presence. An ant walks across my foot, a brief escape from the hot stones. My periwinkle toenails match the blue and white tile in the pool and the mosaic patterns of sea creatures: a lobster, an octopus, a mermaid. In the distance, I can hear the ocean waves crashing on the shore. Our lunch is rice and beans, with salad. *Sabroso!* Delicious, proclaims Abuela—a statement of fact, not opinion. She asks me daily: "Don't you love it here? Isn't it beautiful? I'm so glad we came." No sense of irony, as if it had been her idea in the first place.

She sits quietly on the patio, observes us as we swim. What does she remember? Whom does she know? She knows me and calls me by name, her granddaughter by the daughter of her husband, not hers by blood, hers by sweat and tears and love and time and good fortune or bad. What memories remain of all that she has done, the countries in which she has lived, the homes she settled, the friends she made, the children she raised and the work she accomplished? Or are they gone, evaporated in the humid, tropical air that hangs in the trees and sinks into the mud, absorbed by her skin? There and hers, but hardly accessible.

I show her pictures online—pictures of my house, of my kids, of my garden, 3000 kilometers away—pointing them out, naming them, over and over again. A photo of my mother pops up on the screen. When my aunt told her the news at the time—*Myrta murió*—Abuela repeated it, and then remained silent for the rest of the day. The following day, and the next, she asked, "How is Myrta?" *Fine. She's fine. In Canada.* The response, in essence true, more humane than forcing her to relive the loss over and over again. Now, looking at the photo on the screen,

I search Abuela's face for a sign, an expression, some semblance of recognition. Stillness. Did she wonder who it was? Did she recognize the shape of her eyes, of her head, her smile? Did she have a flash, a moment to think: *that's my girl, my daughter—where is she, why doesn't she come to see me, why doesn't she call?* Perhaps she remembered. Perhaps, without her glasses on, she couldn't even see the face in the photo. I should ask her.

I am getting ready to leave again and wonder when I will return. Will she still be here next time? I watch her, reclined on the sofa, eyes closed, hands crossed over her chest like Cleopatra in her coffin, her hair so thin and white, her face smooth but spotted brown with age. I should ask questions. *What was my mother like as a little girl? Why did you fall in love with Abuelo? Were you disappointed he already had a child? Were you worried about mothering? Do you remember her now? The red-headed, freckled girl who crossed you so many times? "Ay, m'hija, you'll drive me crazy". Is that what you told her time and again? Or did you just say: "You'll see, you'll see when you're a mother, how hard it is." What do you remember?* Or is it kinder not to ask? Kinder to leave those memories buried, undisturbed in the recesses of her mind, in the waves of the ocean or in the soil of the land? They exist, those memories. There are cells that hold them, these memories of people, places and times past, mere sparks in her brain, flashes of recognition and knowledge—everyone she knew, every place she has been, every thought and every question and every dream—captured, like tiny beads in a capsule, waiting to be released, absorbed, digested. *Do you dream when you sleep, Abuela? Are you dreaming now? Of whom, or what, do you dream?*

I remember stories she told me when I was younger: how she raised her brothers and sisters after her father died, and ensured that they all pursued an education; how she navigated the streets of New York as a young social worker in the projects, single and with no fear of alleys, gangsters, or subway stations; how she wrote a book about Caribbean literature; how she and Abuelo worked with the poor in Venezuela and Paraguay, as missionaries, setting up schools and building latrines; what a good husband my grandfather was; how smart my mother and her sisters were; that my mother's birth mother had once written a poem that was published in the newspaper. A handful of stories and memories. Not much to go on, but enough. Together with photos, letters, and my own memories, they will have to suffice, to tide me over until I, too, can no longer remember and it no longer matters.

Her head rolls on the pillow, and she opens her eyes. *Tengo frío.* I'm cold, she says, and wraps herself in a blanket, despite the heat, then returns to napping. I should wake her, make her play cards, do her nails, read a book with me, *do something.* I'll regret having lost this time. I'll regret it when she's gone, when we no longer have time to be together. I watch her as she sleeps. She looks peaceful. Unaware. Unperturbed. I will remember her this way, until... until *I* no longer remember her, or anything. *What do you remember, Abuela? Whom do you recall?*

Perhaps, I, too, will lose touch with my past, with no concept of future, knowing only *now*. One day, I may no longer remember this place, or my own mother, or who, exactly, *I* am. Who will sit with me then? Who will sit and stare at my old body, my skin browning and wrinkled, my hair white as the wisps of cotton on a branch? What will they wonder about me? That person, or those people, who will do this may not even exist yet. I have lived a lifetime, and will live another, before reaching her age, before knowing the generation that will follow my children, before knowing those people who will wonder about me and my life.

She wakes and picks at her nails. In a moment she will ask me where is my aunt and tell me she needs to go to the bathroom. She sits up, calls me by my aunt's name. *Voy al baño*, she announces and swings her bird legs over the edge of the sofa, placing her hand on the coffee table, and then, reconsidering, she reaches for the arm of the sofa. She moves over, closer to the edge, and shuffles forward a little further on her seat. From here, she can grab onto the counter and pull herself upright. *Voy al baño*, she repeats. She rises, and stands, takes one step, then another; deliberate, determined, awkward and graceful at the same time. She moves her four-pronged cane along with her, ahead of her, something for which to reach, but not on which to lean. Step, by step, by step. *Voy al baño*. This is her mission, today and now.

The sun shines through the slatted windows, the shadows of branches wave in the breeze. It is no longer raining, and the air coming in off the street smells fresh and damp. The mango tree in the center of the crescent stands tall. I remember eating mangoes from this tree as a kid, the flesh, sweet; the juice, sticky and dribbling down my chin as I looked up through the branches at the clear blue sky. We are so close to the sun here, always, and don't know when we will simply melt away, what will be left behind. A memory. The heat of the sun.

TAKE A PHOTO BEFORE I LEAVE YOU

BY AMY MACRAE

Click.

I'm caught again. My friend beams at me from behind her phone. "You two are so adorable!" she coos.

I push my daughter on the swing, throw my head back and laugh, mouth open, conscious that I am being watched.

Click.

Another photo, another option, another angle. In case our eyes are closed, perhaps, or in case the pictures don't capture the candidness of the moment in just the right way.

A mother with her daughter.

A loving mother having fun with her daughter.

I know all the reasons these photos are being taken. I know what these photos will be used for and where they will be displayed. But I laugh and smile nevertheless.

My husband, Garreth, rarely used to take photos of me. Usually, he was preoccupied with a beautiful view, intricate architecture, or an exotic car sighting. I'd often poke fun at him for the ridiculous things he would photograph.

"Why the heck do you want a photo of that license plate?" I'd moan. "Are you really going to look at that later?"

"Yeah," he'd reply defensively, scrolling through thousands of little squares in his camera roll. Gargantuan sandwich, limited edition sneakers, lewd graffiti, blurry shot of a deer in the front yard. My default was always to limit photos. I felt it took something away from the experience, seeing life through the lens of a phone. Saving the experience for later, somehow negating the ability to remain in the moment. But Garreth always wanted to collect photos, to store little jokes and bits of beauty to perk himself up on a later day. A grid of colors to scroll through, validating his experiences, making up for his lacklustre memory.

So, when he started collecting images of me, I noticed.

"Is he worried he'll forget me?" I wondered. "Or maybe scared that she will?"

They tell me that I'm different, that I'm stronger, that I'll beat this, that I'll still be here. But they collect photos for when I'm not.

This terrible thing happened to him too. This unbearable loss changed the course of Garreth's life as a child. But this time, he has advance notice. He can make preparations. He can store things for later.

But it isn't just my husband, it's everyone: my parents, my sister, my brother, my friends. I watch them, my senses tuned for the moment when, in the midst of a purely joyful moment, something dawns—their realization that time is limited, but more pressingly, that I am limited—and they reach for their phone.

Mother reading books with daughter in bed.

Happy family collecting berries at the farm.

Two best friends out for a sushi dinner.

Click.

Their actions, their use of the camera, betray their words. They reassure hope at every turn, spew out platitudes and attempt to comfort me with, "No one really knows for sure." They tell me that I'm different, that I'm stronger, that I'll beat this, that I'll still be here. But they collect photos for when I'm not.

After my cancer diagnosis, I started smiling with my teeth. I can't explain why, I just did. Maybe I had been too self-conscious about how I looked before. Maybe it had felt too awkward and revealing, too forward, putting all those teeth out there, opening myself up for the world to see, to judge, to dissect. "Look at her goofy smile," I'd imagine them thinking. "And that kale stuck in her upper incisor." So, I'd always kept my mouth closed, and turned up the corners of my lips, tucked together and tidy.

But after cancer, once it seemed like everything in my life had been ripped open, when everything I had tried so hard to keep neat and contained came spewing out, I smiled with my teeth. I couldn't control my health, I couldn't control my life, so why control my self-image.

I am thirty-four years old, and I've had a rare, incurable form of ovarian cancer for two years. The doctors say I might have one to two years remaining. My daughter, Evie, is four. My daughter, my whole world, not yet old enough to form memories she will carry into adulthood. Will I live long enough to become someone to her—a memory to link along with photographs and stories she's told?

When Evie looks back at all these photos after I'm gone, I wonder who she will see. I wonder what she thinks about the way I look. I know there was another me, a pre-cancer me, but she doesn't. I feel guilt that for most of her conscious life the mom she has known is a sick one. The mom Evie knows spends most of the day in bed while she is cared for by her grandparents. The mom Evie knows ingests more pills than food, can't lift her up, and spends most of her life in pyjamas. For me, this is a bad phase. A dark chapter near the end of the book. But for Evie, this is all there ever was.

I wonder if Evie will know that her mom was a stylish dresser who loved fashion and used it as a language to express herself. Perhaps one day my mom will tell Evie about how I begged to wear a suit to prom. Or maybe Garreth will tell Evie about the brown knee-high fur covered boots I wore on our first date. I don't know why this is important, but it is. Because cancer has taken so much from me, has changed me. But there was someone before her. A girl who had her own style and dressed to the beat of her own drum. Who wasn't afraid to stand out and who was beautiful in a way that she isn't now.

Will I live long enough to become someone to her—a memory to link along with photographs and stories she's told?

Recent images of me could be described as "unfortunate"—and that's generous. I am either bald or with hair in stages of sprouting, awkward in length and texture. Despite my love of fashion, clothes are now purchased for comfort as well as their ability to be quickly stripped off, due to the hot flashes surgical menopause has induced. Multiple surgeries have left my stomach bloated and distended, and a lack of physical activity and courses of steroids through chemo-therapy have left my body soft. A lack of energy and perpetual naps mean make-up is no longer practical or applied.

However, rather than blocking the camera, rather than hiding or putting up verbal opposition, I allow the image to be taken. In fact, I even smile.

When life is coming up to the final bend, perhaps fashion, beauty, and self-image should be the last things one should consider. Dressing well seems like vanity, a frivolousness I can't afford to care about at this point in my life. Yet I have cared. And still do.

Click.

It's Evie's fourth birthday party and all her friends and our family are in attendance. Garreth and I kneel down to align our heads with Evie's, who is poised to inhale her cake. As I bend forward, a curly brown ringlet pops forward and I tuck it back behind my ear.

Made in India, most likely. I read somewhere that that's where most human hair comes from these days. I imagine some poor woman cultivating hair down to her buttocks, sweating under the hot sun for years, only to have it chopped off and shipped across the ocean. My wig is stunning, brunette with shades of blonde and warm tones of honey. It's also excruciatingly hot and itchy and cost as much as a used car. It lives on a stand in my bedroom, tucked away in the corner. There if I need it or want it, which I normally don't.

This particular day, Evie's birthday, it sat ignored while we dressed for the party. Evie and I wore coordinating butterfly print outfits. I despise butterflies, but as far as four-year-old birthday themes go, I suppose she could have done much worse, and I've never been one to shy away from a theme. I made up my face for the occasion and felt a sense of pride as our family of three gathered in the entryway to put on our shoes. Evie looked around to assess the situation.

"Mama, aren't you going to put on your wig?" Evie asked.

I said, no, I wasn't, not today, and that we were ready to go.

"But Mama, don't show my friends your bald head. Put on your wig!"

Garreth went on the defensive. "Evie, Mama looks fine," he pressed.

But I was already dashing down the hallway. "It's fine, it's fine, it's fine, it's fine," was my breathless, calming chant as I wrestled to balance the cap of the wig over my head.

"It's fine," to placate Garreth. "It's fine," to reassure Evie. "It's fine, it's fine, it's fine," to convince myself, my mantra when the life I was living seemed too heavy to bear.

Two hours later, there we were, the three of us, grinning as four candles flickered in the center of a butterfly-shaped cake. Me, with long, wavy hair, the picture of health.

Recorded, eternalized, captured.

But not saved.

CONTRIBUTORS

JULIA SOBRAL CAMPOS is a lifelong lover of words and languages. Born and raised in Rio de Janeiro, Brazil, she attended Sorbonne University (Paris) for her post-secondary education, where she obtained a BA and an MA in Literature. Julia has been working as a literary translator for over a decade and in the last year has started dedicating some of her time to her own writing. She lives in Victoria, BC, with her partner and their two kids.

RAYYA LIEBICH (she/her) is a Canadian writer and educator of Lebanese and Polish descent. She is the author of the award-winning chapbook *Tell Me Everything* (Beret Day Press) and full-length poetry collection *Min Hayati* (Inanna Publications). Passionate about writing as a tool for transformation and changing the discourse on grief, she is currently obsessed with nonlinear forms of Creative Non-Fiction and completing a hybrid memoir on her simultaneous experience of motherhood/mother-loss. She finds joy in teaching creative writing in Nelson, BC.

AMY MARISSA MACRAE (née Ho) was born in Calgary, lived for several years in Toronto (where she met her husband, Garreth) but spent most of her life in Vancouver. Amy was a passionate educator, teaching behavioural special needs kindergarten. Amy was also a tireless, and immensely proud, mother to her 5-year-old daughter, Evie. Amy recently found her voice as a writer and added prose to her repertoire of skills and passions. Amy died on June 1, 2020, at the age of thirty-five. Her story, "Take a Photo Before I Leave You," was shortlisted by the 2020 CBC Nonfiction Prize.

IOANNA SAHAS MARTIN is a public servant at Global Affairs Canada. Publishing credits include articles on international issues and poetry in bywords.ca and Event: Poetry and Prose. She received an honourable mention in the 2022 Gritlit short story contest. Born in Waterloo, Ontario, Ioanna is a first generation Canadian of Greek and Puerto Rican heritage. She resides in Ottawa with her husband and three children.

MARTHA MORRISON holds a Bachelor of Science in Biochemistry from Queen's University and is a recent graduate of the Master of Fine Arts program in Creative Non-Fiction from the University of King's College (Halifax, Canada). Originally from Toronto, Martha worked as a flight attendant and a professional ballroom dance instructor before meeting a farmer who convinced her to leave the city life behind. Now married, they live with their son and two dogs on a farm in rural south western Ontario — and they are expecting a baby girl in the spring.

PETER NEWMAN is a recently retired family physician and teacher of medical residents who has worked in Vancouver, Toronto, the Arctic, Israel, the Golan Heights, Dominica, and Uganda. He received the

2021 Mimi Divinsky Award for Narrative in Family Medicine, and his creative non-fiction has appeared in *Canadian Family Physician, Canadian Medical Association Journal- Humanities, La Presa, Toronto Star,* and *The Globe and Mail.* His memoir, *Heartbeat,* is to be published in 2024. Peter lives in Toronto and Guanajuato, Mexico, and loves skiing, canoeing, hanging out with grandkids...and music.

SUSANNA RANCE is a sociologist, a retired academic based in East London, UK. She spent half her life in La Paz, Bolivia, where her children were born, and returns there often for family visits. She has done freelance journalism in English and Spanish, and has also published some travel writing and poetry. She is now concentrating on memoir, with a book project entitled "Inside The Impossible Mother."

BARCLAY ROSE is an artist who holds a Master's degree in Gender and International Development. She grew up under prairie skies but currently lives with her husband and newborn on Vancouver Island, traditional Coast Salish territory, where they run The Ou Gallery, an artist residency and writing retreat. Barclay is so grateful to help honour Amy's legacy as her mom was a cancer survivor who just passed away from a third battle with the disease. You can see Barclay's work at www.theougallery.com/Barclay or on Instagram @bmmr.ose.

CHERYL SKORY SUMA has a MHSc Speech-Language Pathology and an HBSc Psychology. Cheryl's fiction, creative nonfiction and poetry have appeared in US, UK and Canadian publications, including *Barren Magazine, The Santa Fe Writers' Project, Exposition Review, Reckon Review, Longridge Review, National Flash Fiction Day, Fatal Flaw Literary, Blank Spaces Magazine, Pulp Literature* and many others, and her work placed in thirty-one competitions across 2019-22. She recently joined the team at *Reckon Review* as a staff reader. You can find her on twitter @CherylSkorySuma

---

DANA WEBSTER is an observational blog writer, memoirist, and creative short fiction writer. She might also have a novel or two in the works. She resides in Mono, Ontario, with her husband and five rescue cats.

SHARON WHITE was born and raised on the Caribbean island of Trinidad and educated in Trinidad, France, and Canada, where she has been residing for the last twenty years. Her professional interests have always been in multicultural and multilingual environments as her positions at the Inter-American Development Bank (1989-2001) and the Royal Academy of Dance (2002-2006) attest. In 2006, when she moved permanently to Canada, Sharon went back to university and became TESL qualified. Shortly after, she joined the International English Program at the University of Manitoba and taught English to international students for eight years. She is now retired from teaching and living in Montreal.

2022 JUDGE

ELIZABETH ROSNER is an American novelist, nonfiction author, essayist, and poet. Her three novels have been awarded literary prizes in both the US and Europe, including the Harold U. Ribalow Prize and the Prix France Bleu Gironde, as well as being shortlisted for the prestigious Prix Femina and selected for 'best books' lists by the San Francisco Chronicle and National Public Radio. Her stunning book of nonfiction, *Survivor Café*, blends memoir with research on intergenerational trauma. It was a finalist for the National Jewish Book Award.

Rosner's essays have appeared in the NY Times Magazine, Elle, Hadassah Magazine, the Huffington Post, and numerous anthologies. She travels widely to lead intensive writing workshops, to lecture on contemporary literature, and to visit with book groups.

AMY AWARD FOUNDER

ALISON WEARING is a Canadian writer, playwright, and performer. Her writing has won a National Magazine Award Gold Medal, been a finalist for the Journey Prize, nominated for the RBC Taylor Prize, shortlisted for the Edna Staebler Award for Creative Nonfiction, and her books have become national bestsellers. Her numerous theatre awards include Best Dramatic Script at New York City's United Solo, the largest festival of solo theatre in the world.

Alison's current project, *Memoir Writing Ink.*, is an interactive online program that guides people through the process of transforming personal stories into memoir. In her spare time, Alison is a devoted hiker, yogi, and cultivator of laughter.

THE STORY BEHIND
THE AMY AWARD

In May 2019, a group of writers met at the Mindful Memoir retreat in southern France. Among them was a sparkling young woman named Amy. I believe I speak for everyone in the group when I say that we all instantly loved her spunk and spirit, her honesty and tender heart.

The writing Amy presented during the retreat was spectacular, and she spoke often of her daughter, then four years old, and her husband Garreth (who, among other things, surprised her with a bouncy castle at their wedding—the photo of Amy and her bridesmaids bouncing in their dresses might be the most beautiful wedding photo I've ever seen). Amy also spoke of her work as a kindergarten teacher, which she adored, and of her cancer, the terminal diagnosis she had been given a year earlier, and how deeply she wanted to write her story, to give life to her voice on the page.

On the last night of the retreat, Amy gave us all glow sticks and we followed her in dancing around the living room of the château to her favourite tunes. It was crazily fun. The next morning, Clara (with whom I facilitate the France retreats) and I took everyone to the train station and we waved like maniacs from the platform as Amy sped away to Paris, where she would catch her flight home to Vancouver.

Over the ensuing months, Amy worked hard revising and polishing one of the pieces she had written in France. "Do you really think it could be published," she asked me at one point, "or are you just being nice?"

I assured her I was being honest, that her writing was strong and pure, simple and majestic, but I'm not sure she ever believed me. The best writers often don't.

On June 1, 2020, at the age of thirty-five, Amy died of ovarian cancer.

A few weeks later, the CBC contacted the writers whose stories had been selected as finalists for their prestigious annual literary awards. Amy MacRae was one of five writers shortlisted for the CBC Nonfiction Prize.

In the ensuing months, I thought of Amy a lot. Sometimes I would 'bring her with me' on hikes, her presence a reminder of how fortunate I was to have a body healthy enough to scale a rock face, skip over tree roots, or just close my eyes and listen to the wind peel a layer of water from the surface of the lake.

Amy taught me to see every grey hair as a privilege, every interaction as an opportunity for kindness, and every morning as an offering, even in the midst of a lockdown.

One afternoon, in the depths of winter, I was snowshoeing through the forest with Amy in my heart, when I had an idea. Or rather, Amy passed me an idea. Or rather, she pressed a thought into the shape of a snowflake, blew it off a high branch and let it spiral down and land on my nose, at which point I smiled and looked up, blinked a few times, and felt as if I had an idea. (Pick your preferred understanding of inspiration.)

The idea was to create a literary contest in Amy's honour and donate the proceeds to her living legacy fund for ovarian cancer research.

Thus, the *International Amy MacRae Award for Memoir* was born.

This was the second year of the contest, and this the second anthology, and I look forward to many more.

May it be a source of inspiration. And a celebration of Amy, for inspiring us all.

with a hand over my heart,

Alison

Alison Wearing

CPSIA information can be obtained
at www.ICGtesting.com
Printed in the USA
LVHW101130080423
743800LV00003BA/73

9 781778 140228